author's note

Mathematickles! is a brain tickler. It teases your brain by mixing together math and language. Fun words are written in place of numbers in all sorts of math problems—addition, subtraction, multiplication tables, division, fractions, geometry, and more. There are graphs of a snowball fight and an inchworm climbing a branch. Baby-bird beaks become angles and so do twirling seed pods. Just open your mind as the book leads you down a brand new path, on which math becomes fun, silly, beautiful, easy, and creative. You'll find that the seasons tie all the poems together, starting with the first signs of fall and ending with the last breeze of summer. Once you've read this book, I bet you won't be able to resist writing a few math poems of your own.

poems by Betsy Franco + illustrations by Steven Salerno =

Mathematickles!

MARGARET K. McELDERRY BOOKS   NEW YORK   LONDON   TORONTO   SYDNEY   SINGAPORE

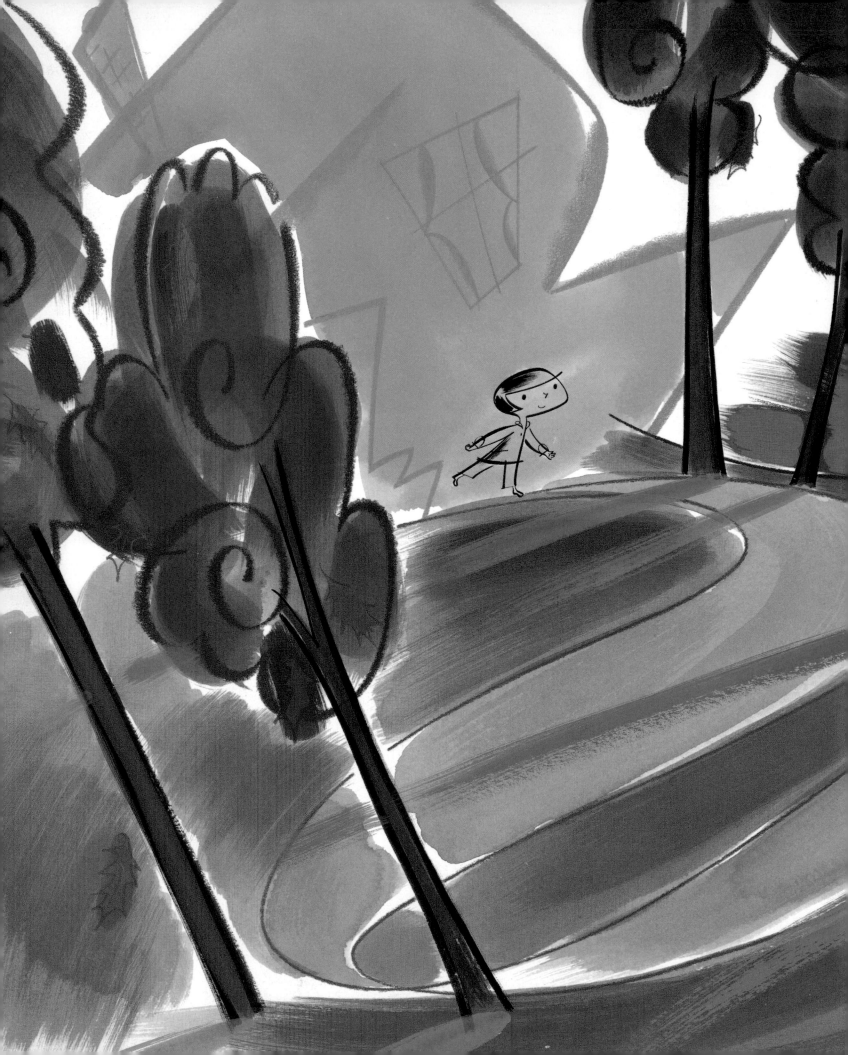

crisp air
shadows tall
+ cat's thick coat
—————————————
signs of fall

nest

- bird
_____

stringfeatherstwigsleaves

squirrels + _____ = winter storage

No

holes + nuts - nuts = squirrel hide & seek

$$\frac{\text{pumpkin patch} \times \text{sunlight}}{\text{oooooooooooorange!}}$$

pumpkin - seeds + face = jack-o'-lantern

red
orange
gold
+ brown
_____
crunchy rainbow on the ground

$$\frac{1}{2}w = v = \text{flying geese}$$

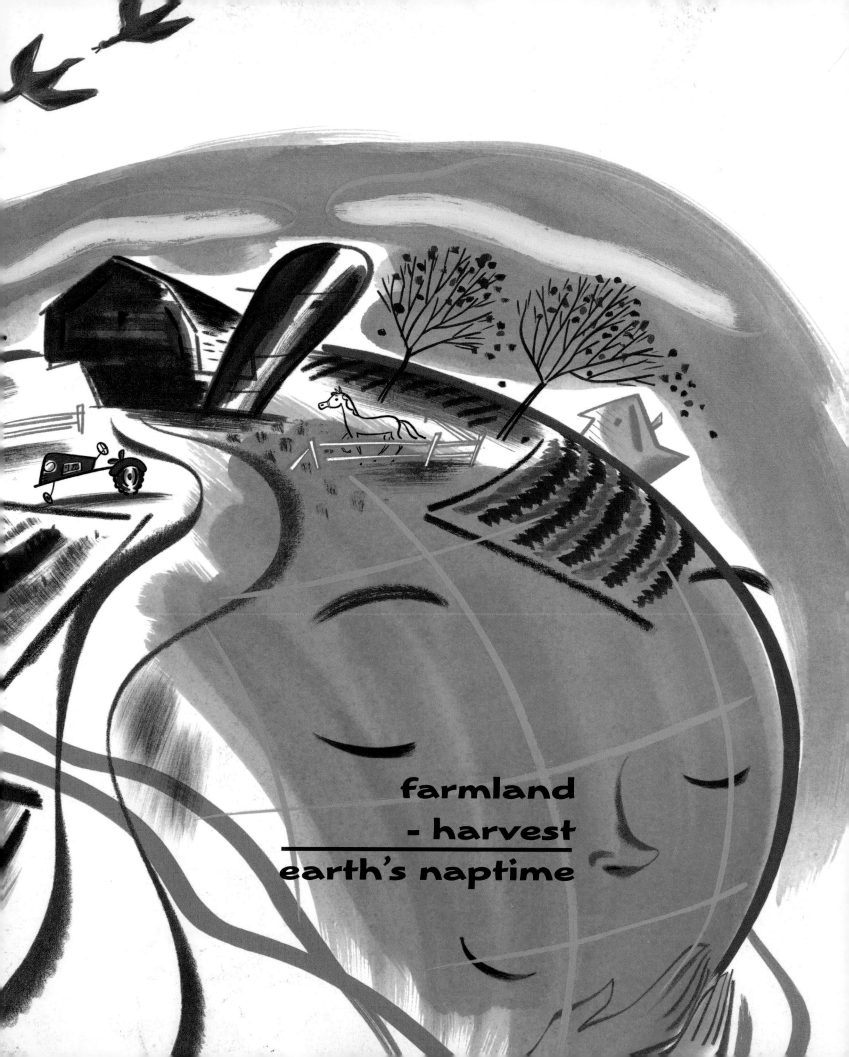

farmland
- harvest
earth's naptime

hexagons
x frozen lace
——————————
snow flurry

ice puddle + snow boot = creakgroanCRACK!

$$\frac{\text{rooftops} + \text{first snow}}{\text{white blanket}}$$

Preparing for a Snowball Fight

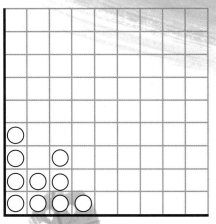

Snowball Fight

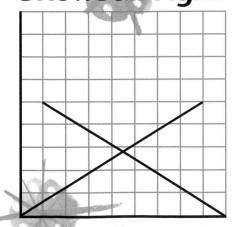

sphere
sphere
+ sphere
_____
snowman

Sledding

X	cold	sun
snow	snow	slush
rain	sleet	rainbow
window	frost	sunbeam

sneeze x 3 = winter sniffles

threads
stitches
triangles
+ squares
_____
winter quilt made with care

kitten + leaves + branches - meow = pussy willow

croak
croak
CROAK
+ rrribit
_____
a knot of toads

$$\frac{\text{raindrops} \times \text{leaves}}{\text{pearls on green plates}}$$

Frogs Playing Leapfrog

baby birds de√ouring worms

Inchworm Climbing a Branch

tulips x daffodils = spring garden

Bird Taking Flight

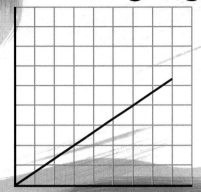

t〰〰irling seedpods

Butterfly Dance

clover
+ knots
―――――――――
springnecklace

pelican diving for fish

pelican diving for fish

$$\text{time} \overline{) \text{ocean}}$$
$$\begin{array}{r} \text{waves} \\ \text{time} \overline{) \text{ocean}} \\ - \text{rhythm} \\ \hline \text{spray} \end{array}$$

rocks x waves = sand

hammock
shade
+ lemonade
perfectly lazy summer day

rrrrr

Cat Jumping
for a Butterfly

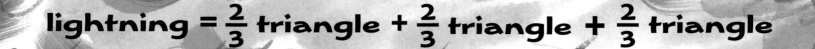

lightning $= \frac{2}{3}$ triangle $+ \frac{2}{3}$ triangle $+ \frac{2}{3}$ triangle

rrrummble

Z Boom!

$$\begin{array}{l} \text{thunder} \\ \text{lightning} \\ \text{wind} \\ + \text{ rain that's warm} \\ \hline \text{summer storm} \end{array}$$

late summer
x cool air
———————————
first fall breeze

soft pillow
sleepyhead
+ clean white sheets
———————————
time for bed

lightningbugs x jar = summer lantern

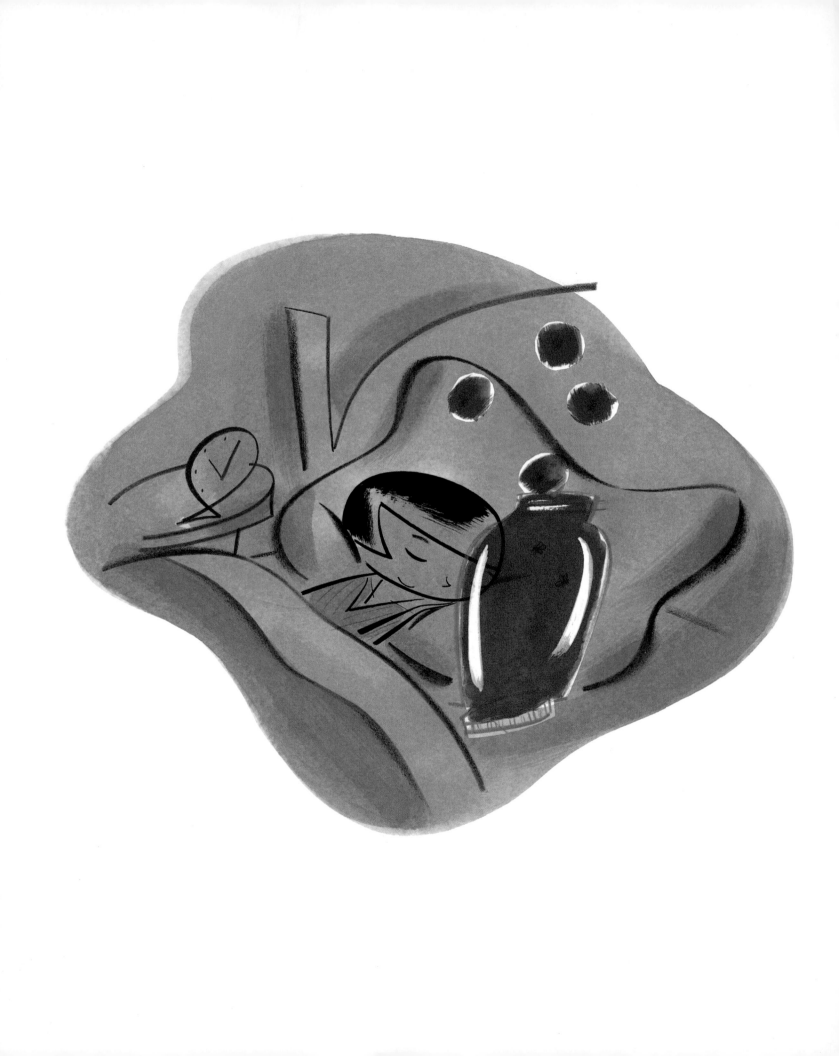

For James, Thomas, and David
I am very grateful to Bob Grumman, whose poetry inspired this collection.
Thank you as well to Justin Ellerby, who helped me brainstorm the title.
—B. F.

For Debby, Christy, Joey, and Tony, and our seasons together
—S. S.

Margaret K. McElderry Books
An imprint of Simon & Schuster Children's Publishing Division
1230 Avenue of the Americas
New York, NY 10020

Book design by Sonia Chaghatzbanian
The text of this book is set in Havergal.
The illustrations are rendered in watercolor and gouache.

Manufactured in China

2 4 6 8 10 9 7 5 3

Library of Congress Cataloging-in-Publication Data
Franco, Betsy.
Mathematickles / Betsy Franco ; illustrated by Steven Salerno.
p. cm.
Summary: A collection of poems written in the form of mathematical
problems and grouped according to seasonal themes.
ISBN 0-689-84357-7
1. Mathematics—Juvenile poetry. 2. Children's poetry, American. [1. Mathematics—Poetry.
2. Seasons—Poetry. 3. American poetry. 4. Visual poetry.] I. Salerno, Steven, ill. II. Title.
PS3556.R3325 M37 2003
811'.54—dc21
2001055844

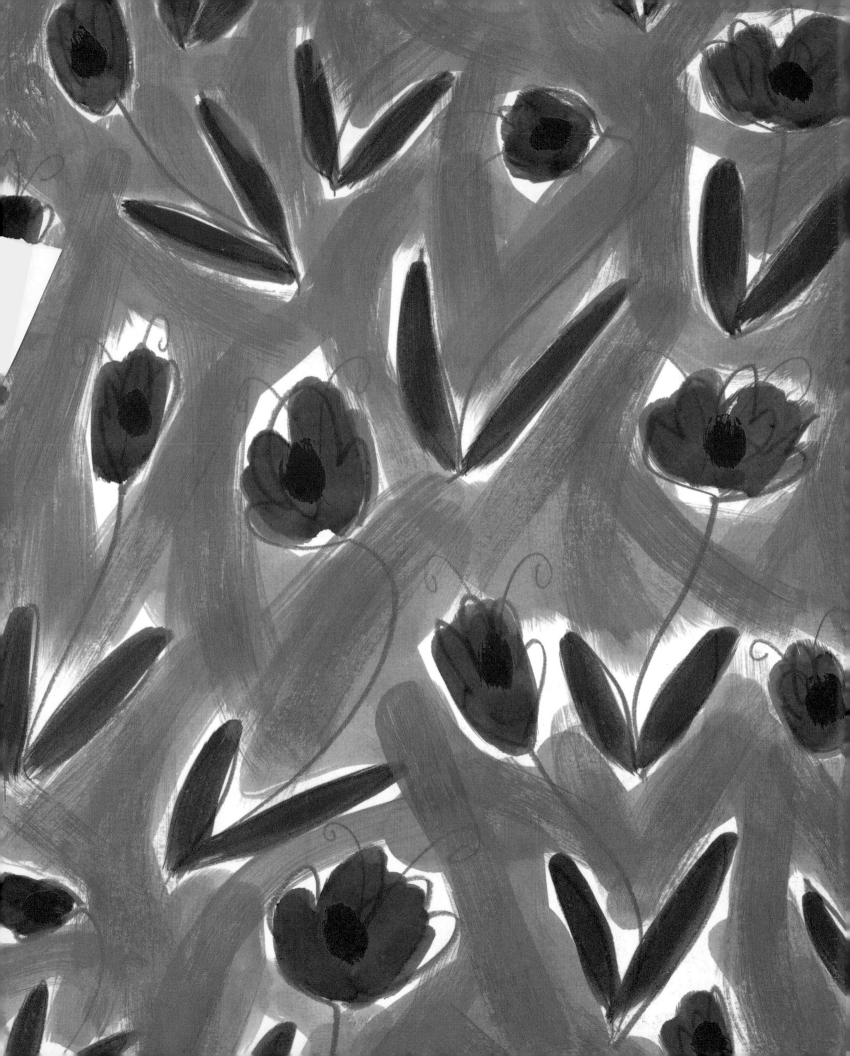